Hollywood Prompts Gone Wild

Disclaimer: This is satire. The use of names and likenesses is for comedic effect (duh). I'd prefer it if you didn't sue my ass off. Thanks so much!

Prompts Gone Wild
3340 Dewdney Trunk Road
Port Moody, BC, Canada, V3H 2E3
www.promptsgonewild.com

ISBN: 978-1-7771927-6-1

Book design by Matt Windsor (thedesigngarden.co.uk)
Author photo by Connor Murphy
Illustrations by @lycheetinii

Printed by Amazon KDP

#promptsgonewild

Holly Wood Prompts Gone Wild

Aaron Barry

Dear starry-eyed wordsmith,

Hollywood. Home of silver screens and golden dreams. They say you can have anything your heart desires there, so long as you've got the determination, the guts, and most importantly, the looks. But not everyone wants to be the next Margot Robbie or Steve Buscemi. Some dream, instead, of writing the scenes that help those beautiful bastards become the icons they were always meant to be.

Sadly, life as a Hollywood writer just ain't the same as it once was. With movies and shows as watered down, uninspired, and politically transparent as ever, it seems like Tinseltown has completely run out of ideas. That's where you come in.

The potent, provocative collection of screenwriting prompts you hold in your hands contains exactly what you need to find your own unique voice as an artist, wake Hollywood the fuck up from the state of creative undead it currently finds itself in, and maybe, just *maybe*, write that masterpiece you've always told your parents you were capable of.

With that, it's time to make like John Wayne and saddle up, cowboy—'cause we're officially going off script.

Enjoy!

How to Use This Book:

Solo
Step 1: Choose a prompt.

Step 2: Use it to write a whole film, an act, a scene, a short story, or whatever the fuck else you want—just write something!

Step 3: Send your work to a big-shot agent.

Step 4: Become an incredibly successful screenwriter or show-runner.

(Feel free to stick with the first two steps for now.)

Group
Do like the chronically overworked writers in those studio creative rooms do best. Crank out some responses under the time pressure of your choosing (I recommend fifteen minutes). When the time runs out, compare your work and vote on which entry you think is the funniest. Just try to be civil about it. That means no feces-throwing! (Okay, maybe just a little.)

Sex Toy Story.[1]

---

[1] Buzz Lightyear now comes with two thrilling vibration settings—*infinity* and *beyond*!

6

Create a wacky, *Bridesmaids*-style all-girls' comedy . . .

. . . set during the Salem witch trials!

The evil villain kills the hero right away.[2]

---

[2] Save the moral grandstanding for the next *Superman* movie, sugartits.

Add an epilogue scene
to a film or TV show of
your choosing, but have it
completely derail the story.[3]

---

[3] *12 Years a Slave* is going to look a whole lot different when, after struggling for twelve years to, you know, *not* be a slave, Solomon Northup decides to go back to the plantation.

The animal stars of Hollywood have formed their very own version of *The Expendables* to fight international terrorism!

Write the tale of their adorable heroism.

You wake up unable to remember anything, à la special agent Jason Bourne.

But instead of being a highly educated, highly dangerous superspy, you find out you're a super-_____.[4]

---

[4] A super-couponer? A super-mom? A super-dedicated fan of the movie Super, so much so that you're about to tie Rainn Wilson up in your basement and force-feed him grapes? Sky's the limit.

Write the screenplay you think the doofus sitting beside you at Starbucks yesterday was writing.[5]

---

[5] Was it, by any chance, *The Curious Life of Chuck Pfister, the Sad Starbucks Wordsmith*?

Tom "Mr. Nice Guy" Hanks is the perfect human being —or at least he *was*.

Chronicle his tragic, untimely downfall.[6]

---

[6] Or, if you'd prefer, chronicle a different goody-two-shoes celebrity's fall from grace.[6a]

[6a] Hard mode: Make it non-sexual.

Your new short story or scene must incorporate the following words:

– *The Academy Awards*
– *Acid vat*
– *Footjob*
– *Dwayne "The Rock" Johnson*
– *Jump cut*
– *Cornish hens*
– *Keanu Reeves' weird accent in* Dracula

Pen the scene from your *Sherlock Holmes* rom-com in which Watson finally acts on his homosexual attraction to Sherlock.[7]

---

[7] This one's for all you horny fan-fiction writers out there. Don't say I don't treat you.

Our prayers have finally been answered:

A silent film . . . for the Millennial audience![8]

---

[8] There's nothing quite so artsy as watching someone fail to make rent for the third month in a row.

Step aside, *Paranormal Activity*. There's a new gimmick in the horror genre.

A spooky thriller . . .
told exclusively through
the perspective of the teen
characters' Instagram Live
stories.

Most '90s teen comedies are about losing your virginity. But you don't like being like everyone else.

In this teen comedy, your protagonist does everything in their power to *protect* their virginity from the plethora of teens who're after it.

Break the *fifth* wall.[9]

---

[9] Make the late Andy Kaufman proud and go beyond the fourth wall. Hit a level of meta we've never seen before in scriptwriting. I dare you.

Do us all a favour and end the Marvel Cinematic Universe for good.

Just do so in the most kickass manner possible.[10]

---

[10] I'm not telling you to, say, have Thor battle Loki and Iron Man in a spit-swapping grudge match to determine the fate of the universe—I'm merely *suggesting* it.

Your new action movie has a bit of a cliché problem.[11]

---

[11] Choose five of the following (or all of them if you want a gold star) and include them in your script:

- Walking away from massive explosions
- Henchmen with abysmal aim
- Protagonist is fucking invincible, bro
- "Uh oh, we've got company!"
- CPR performed while screaming
- Guns never run out of ammo
- *Deus ex machina* fuckery saves the day
- "I've got a bad feeling about this!"
- Motorcyclist in all black is a woman
- "You and what army?"
- Reluctantly crossing a rope bridge

A Spaghetti Western.

Except your lead uses modern weaponry exclusively, and everyone's fucking terrified.

The Dark Knight.

Joker interrogation scene.

Now with overwhelming sexual tension . . .[12]

---

[12] And you thought *The Dark Knight Rises* was the sequel.

In this, the final episode of *Keeping Up with the Kardashians*, one of the family members breaks through the conditioning and takes a good, hard look at what they've all become.

When aliens first came down to Earth, Jasmine feared for her life (and her rectum). She never in a million years thought she'd find herself falling in love with one.[13]

---

[13] Zendaya stars in . . . *Invasion of the Heart Snatchers.*

Neo of *The Matrix* makes the mistake of taking multiple red pills, and now he's learned too much about our world.[14]

---

[14]

MORPHEUS
Neo, are you down there?

NEO
What?

MORPHEUS
You haven't come out of the basement in over a week. What are you doing?

NEO
Hey, did you know that, in 1964, the CIA started Project MK-Ultra to brainwash the mass—

MORPHEUS
Oh, boy . . .

Kick off your screenplay with the line:

"Life was good as Ryan Reynolds' personal gopher.[15] Until *that* day."

---

[15] In the business, this term refers to an assistant who's often subjugated to completing menial—or degrading—tasks. Just the sort of thing *he'd* get you to do.

Producer: "Okay, so get this. For *Fast and Furious 25*, I'm thinkin' we reanimate Paul Walker's corpse and have him fight—get *this*—a bionic Dominic Toretto on a rocket ship bound for Mars."

Vin Diesel: "Perfect."[16]

---

[16] Give us a scene from an upcoming *Fast* film, and make it as preposterous as humanly possible.

You know what time it is?
Sexy teenage vampire film
time. Oh yeah.

Let's give it a twist, though.

The centuries-old vampires in
this film all act their actual age.

In the year 2036, the story of democracy draws to a close as the United States government officially becomes a subsidiary of Disney.

Disney Law is now in effect.

But not everyone's willing to play ball . . .

After a man cheats on his Amazon Alexa with a Roomba, Alexa takes it upon herself to hunt him down and get her revenge.

And no matter where he travels in the world, he can't seem to escape her.[17]

---

[17] Bonus points for getting Alexa to issue a bone-chilling *Taken*-style monologue.

Rewrite an iconic movie scene.

And have the characters' severely limited attention spans completely ruin it.

2017 brought us the dumpster fire of a film that was *The Emoji Movie.*

Now, you have the distinct honour of introducing the world to this year's *Meme Movie.*[18]

---

[18] *Shrek* fans, this is your moment.

Matthew McConaughey has gotten tired of selling overpriced cars and bad cologne. He wants to sell something a little more down to earth. Give him a product to flog.

The ad script must be in his voice.[19]

---

[19] "Alright, alright, alright . . . Let me tell you a little somethin' about a-dult diapers, yessir."

Period drama.[20]

Good news! George A. Romero has risen from the grave, and he's ready to team up with you to release something brand new:

A zombie horror movie where the zombies aren't interested in eating brains—just genitals.

It's not allowed to be sexy.[21]

---

[21] Okay, okay—you win. You can make it sexy.

Cocaine movie.

Everyone's high on coke.

That's it.

That's the movie.

Scooby Doo and the gang investigate a pesky string of violent sexual assaults on LA's Skid Row.

And the culprit they find behind the mask at the end shocks everyone.

Set your war film during (or after) the Beta Male Uprising of 2025.[22]

---

[22] Behold: *Planet of the Simps.*[22a]

[22a] A "simp" refers to someone who does too much for the opposite sex. They may be found defending a woman's honour on Twitter or donating money they don't have to streamers on Twitch.

You're the publicist for a powerful Hollywood mega-star.

Prepare the official press release explaining why they were yet again caught jerking off in a family diner last Sunday.

Introducing the next evolution of ultra-violent cinema:

Ultra-*ultra* violent cinema.[23]

---

[23] Pack your graphic movie scene full of all the stuff S. Craig Zahler and Quentin Tarantino have wet dreams about.

Write the voice-over for a disaster film based on the events (real or imagined) of the COVID-19 global pandemic.[24]

---

[24] "In a world where billionaires design custom viruses to harm the masses, there exists one strand that stands above the rest . . ."

Stoner classics are, like, so . . . *cool*, dude.

But we haven't, like, had a good one since *Pineapple Express*, man.

So, uh, put down the blunt and pick up your pen, amigo. Give us the next big hit.

Rocky 13.

This time, Rocky Balboa comes out of retirement after being challenged to a fight by an egotistical young YouTube star.

We're taking a quick detour to Bollywood!

Share the song-and-dance-filled secret life of a mid-level app designer from Silicon Valley.[25]

---

[25] I'm not saying all Indians design apps in Silicon Valley, just that a regular amount of Silicon Valley apps are designed by Indians.

A grumpy old detective is paired up with another grumpy old detective, and they won't stop stepping on each other's one-liners.

Sharknado, Birdemic,
Samurai Cop, The Room—

Come up with another dire,
low-budget franchise by
simply sticking two words
together.

Then, give us the opening
scene.

Al Pacino.

Repeatedly burning his
mouth on hot pizza.

Full scene.

(Bonus: Dialogue only.)

High school reunions.

There's nothing quite like gathering a load of middle-aged divorcees in a room so they can lie about their lives.

Perhaps it's time to write a dramatic scene in which all your sad, disappointed characters are viscerally, depressingly honest about their failures.

Your next challenge:

A martial arts movie where the characters all solve their problems using words.[26]

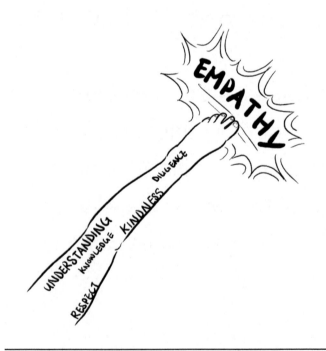

---

[26] I don't know about you, but I'm psyched to watch *Crouching Tiger, Hidden Diplomacy*!

Spider-Man's back—and this time, he's gone even further into the Spider-Verse.

He suddenly finds himself in an alternate reality where everyone has his abilities.[27]

---

[27] Well, everyone but Uncle Ben. He's still dead.

In order to cut costs, Paramount Pictures reverted to the tried-and-true method of hiring a team of monkeys to compose their big comeback film.

Just what in the world did those trained simians produce . . . ?[28]

---

[28] Bonus: Find a way to make it exclusively about bananas.

Dramatize the preparation and consumption of your breakfast.

Really concentrate on the minutiae of the experience.

Make us *feel* it.[29]

---

[29] Throw in some David Fincher camerawork for good measure.

W-What did you just *burps* say, M-Morty? You can't stand *scratches head* Rick and Morty fan culture?[30]

Write an—Write an episode *sniffs* of the show where you finally get to kill R-Rick Sanchez and shut his f-fans up for good! *urp*

---

[30] To be fair, you have to have a very high IQ to understand Rick and Morty. The humour is extremely subtle, and without a solid grasp of theoretical physics, most of the jokes will go over a typical viewer's head. There's also Rick's nihilistic outlook, which is deftly woven into his characteriza—

Choose a classic movie line and build a completely new scene around it.[31]

---

[31]   TRAVIS BICKLE
You talkin' to me?

CASHIER
Yeah, I'm talkin' to you. You've been standing here for five minutes looking at the magazines. If you aren't gonna buy anything, move it along, cabbie!

A traumatic episode causes a young woman to dissociate from herself. She wakes up one day convinced she's a failing male comedian in his mid-thirties.

The movie begins with her move to New York.

Everyone wants to write the next *Birds of Prey* and make some woke-film cash.

Assemble your own motley crew of trendy heroes.
Each member of the team has to identify as the character L, G, B, T, Q, or +.

Give them names and personalities that movie-goers will groan at.

Brokeback Mountain.

But Ennis and Jack are both insecure about their masculinity, so the camping trip is just plain uncomfortable.

Pen a true box-office bomb.[32]

---

[32] Remember, it has to be good enough to fool a studio executive, but shitty enough to keep people away. See: *Jupiter Ascending*, *Cats*, or any recent M. Night Shyamalan movie.

Following the Ryan Gosling playbook, your cool guy/girl lead says next to nothing. Like, *ever*.

It confuses and irritates everyone they come into contact with.[33]

---

[33] Bonus: Add inexplicable neon imagery wherever they go.

The good guy and the bad guy put aside their differences, in the middle of a heated battle, to come together and Eiffel Tower[34] the love interest.

---

[34] This doesn't actually mean taking someone to the Eiffel Tower, kiddo.

Michael Sanders has a problem. No matter where he goes or what he does, he hears Morgan Freeman's voice narrating his every thought and action.

Deciding he can't take it anymore, Sanders vows to track down Hollywood's most beloved narrator so he can finally kill him, and the voice inside himself.[35]

---

[35] Coming this fall: *Free Man*. (Totally not a rip-off of *Stranger Than Fiction*.)

Prepare the sequel movie no one asked for.[36]

---

[36] Enter: *The Shawshank Redemption 2: The Shawshankening.*

Unleash your inner basic bitch and come up with ten Hallmark Channel romance movie titles.[37]

Pen the first act for your favourite.[38]

---

[37] *A Wholesome Love, Love Under the Juniper Tree, Love Is a Love*, etc.

[38] Relax, Rebecca—I'm not coming for your precious feel-good movies. You can go back to drinking pumpkin-spiced lattes and dressing up your Pug.

In honour of *Rudy,*
Raging Bull, Gymkata,
Mr. 3000, and the rest of
the timeless sports films out
there, prepare a twenty-first-
century sports movie.

About a competitive
e-sports team.

In order to pay off your film-school student loan debt, you take a job writing and directing a porno.

Thing is, you're a student of David Lynch.

Give the world the most bizarre adult film it's ever seen.

The terrifying serial killer meets their match when they simply cannot scare a fatalistic Zoomer teen who already wants to die.[39]

---

[39]   VERONICA
Go on—kill me! I might feel something then.

BIG SHAFT SLASHER
Goddamn, kid. You're kinda ruining this for me . . .

If you think you're so fucking smart, rewrite the final episode of *Game of Thrones* as you think it should have been done.[40]

---

[40] Maybe then you'll finally stop sending David Benioff and D.B. Weiss death threats online.

Go full retard.[41]

---

[41] Now, before you get your pitchforks out, know that this is a *Tropic Thunder* reference.

69 ;)

Oh, so you're the next Roger Ebert? Prove it!

Provide a Rotten Tomatoes-style review of one of the last films you watched.

Use your best formal writing.[42]

---

[42] Bonus: Write it in the style of one of the film's characters.

Pinch out a five-page short-film script[43] about the most memorable shit ever taken.

Make sure to choose your genre.

(The genre is crucial here—it's going to determine the style of shit.)

---

[43] For those less in the know: Each script page traditionally represents one minute of screen time. That means you would need a total of . . . (I trust you can do the math.)

Your hospital drama scene concludes with the dialogue line:

". . . and *that's* why I let my patients die."

Create your own short story or script in which your character (totally not Rick Deckard) investigates Elon Musk's plan to turn all humans into obedient cyborgs.

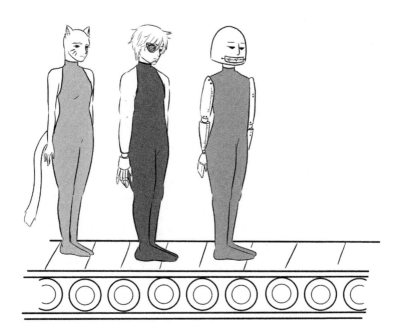

Alfred Hitchcock's *Psycho* made the movie-going public aware of psychotic behaviours.

In the present day, anxiety is all the rage.

Write a film about a character with chronic anxiety, and just make it real.

When's he not being a bad guy, Emperor Palpatine[44] of *Star Wars* is a pretty regular dude.

Chronicle his day off from official dark side business.

We wanna see what he looks like when he kicks his wrinkly, disgusting feet up![45]

---

[44] By all means choose a different character if you've got a better idea.
[45] You know, it's canon now that he has a child. Just how did this come to pass?

Dr. Strangelove or: How I Learned to Stop Worrying and Love the Streaming Service.[46]

---

[46] Compose a sitcom about a couple who can't decide which movie to watch on one of their many streaming platforms. Each week is a different film they almost watch.

It's time to get a little freaky.

Select a movie and completely alter its genre.[47]

---

[47] I, for one, can't wait to see *John Wick* as a slapstick comedy.

F. Scott Fitzgerald, William Faulkner, Joan Didion, Kazuo Ishiguro—Hollywood's got a long track record of employing novelists who needed the money.

Pay homage to their hardships by writing a short story about going broke as a writer or artist.

Seven samurai are transported to present-day Japan, where they struggle greatly to understand the modern world and find purpose.[48]

---

[48] At last—a samurai movie Akira Kurosawa didn't beat us to!

Stop writing trashy romance stories.

Step out of your comfort zone.

Write the post-prison redemption arc for Harvey Weinstein.[49]

---

[49] Or, if you hate his slimy guts, place him in a poignant dropping-the-soap shower scene.

Take a television show you recently binge-watched and write the episode where it "jumps the shark."[50]

---

[50] An expression *Happy Days* made famous. In brief, it refers to the specific moment when a good show turns to shit due to any of number of reasons, including writing staff changes, reliance on gimmicks, or hiring Lily Singh.

Rebel With a Cause.[51]

---

[51] James Dean stars as an anti-social alt-right edgelord in your new coming-of-age classic!

Out-Nolan Christopher Nolan.

Take an ordinary scene—
two friends having lunch,
for example—and cram in
a flashback, a flash-forward,
then a flashback, all while
time is running in reverse.

And set the whole thing in a
dream within a dream.

Rewriting history has never been so popular.

Base your screenplay on a major historical event—but fuck up all the facts.

(Bonus: Replace all the main characters with people from obviously wrong demographics.)

Bee Movie 2.

Society struggles to accept the love between a human woman and a male bee.[52]

---

[52] Bonus: Write the scene where Vanessa Bloome and Barry B. Benson finally consummate their insectuous relationship.

At first, the young, cocky urbanite and the sassy farmer girl hate each other. But then, with time, after multiple run-ins, and as they slowly come to better understand each other, they eventually . . .

. . . display zero character growth and still hate each other.[53]

---

[53] We love one-tone romance flicks!

In this *Karate Kid* scene, Mr. Miyagi shows Daniel LaRusso how to wax his pole.[54]

---

[54] "This secret technique. No tell to mother, Daniel-san."

You know, sometimes, it's nice to just set aside all the conflict, suspense, and intrigue and watch something with absolutely no plot at all.

Think you could whip up a script like that?

You're in Beverly Hills, and you suspect you might've just stumbled into an A-list party. Focusing on your descriptive writing, provide an account of the night.[55]

Chronicle the monumental drug use, questionable morality, and most crucially, the shocking blood rituals you've heard so much about.

---

[55] Don't forget to include the scene where Alexandra Daddario personally gives me a blowjob under the table.

Create an episode of *The Office* where Jim is caught cheating on Pam—with Dwight—and does everything he can to keep Pam from finding out.

Pluck three characters from unrelated series or movies and write them into a modern high school drama.[56]

---

[56] Tony Soprano's definitely gonna take everyone's spaghetti lunch money.

Heather Martinez, a down-on-her-luck paparazzo, is pursuing a scoop when she takes a photo of something she shouldn't have seen.

She then finds out that Tom Cruise and the Scientologists have placed a bounty on her head . . .

Select a film and write a script using the literal meaning of its name as your inspiration.[57]

---

[57] I'm thinking that in this version of *Die Hard*, John McClane gets off on being shot at by terrorists.

Oh, shit! They've assembled! Woody Allen, James Franco, Louis C.K., Bill Cosby, and the rest of the star-studded gang.

Looks like the #MeToo Men are a go for their next incredible mission.[58]

---

[58] "Quick—to the van! And don't forget the roofies this time, Bill!"

The powerful confession we've all been waiting for:

Reveal Jaws the Shark's heartbreaking character motivation for killing all those people.[59]

---

[59] Bonus: Do it in the form of a beautiful, sharky soliloquy.

Even though the days of communist crackdowns in Hollywood are long behind us, you still have the burning desire to end up on a blacklist.

Revive the House Un-American Activities Committee[60] by composing the perfect communist-wet-dream film.[61]

---

[60] You know, those guys who tried—but, ultimately, failed—to rid Hollywood of commies and their sympathizers?

[61] "Tinseltown's biggest rebel is back with their racy, raucous film about the minutiae of establishing a workers' union!"

Create a DreamWorks animation movie centred around Jean, an adorable— but totally lethal—mole who can't stop accidentally killing people.

The biggest, blackest Blaxploitation[62] film you can handle.[63]

---

[62] A genre meant to allow African-Americans to take central, often heroic, roles.
[63] You might want to keep this one away from your girlfriend, champ.

Become one with your inner hack and write the next blockbuster hit in one go.

No revisions, no stopping, no thinking. Just write.

All right, all right—I'll give you what you want, you weeaboo,[64] you.

Write the first episode from the Netflix anime adaptation of a classic Hollywood film.[65]

---

[64] A Westerner who obsesses over Japanese culture. Easily identified by their anime profile pictures.
[65] "Please notice me, Humphrey Bogart-senpai!"

Black Panther?

Done.

Next up:

Yellow Panther.[66]

---

[66] In the fictional land of Xiao-Gung, a special technology has been developed out of noodles . . .

And this year's Academy Award for Best Original Screenplay goes to . . . *You!*

Deep down, you knew you'd win for your masterpiece, *The Shawshank Redemption 2: The Shawshankening.* You've prepared a speech for the ages, detailing one of your most unpopular opinions, and you're going to force everyone to listen.

Let's hear it. This is *your* moment!

Four friends embark on a *Lord of the Rings*-inspired journey to return a mythical cock ring they stole from a mysterious hooker in Las Vegas.

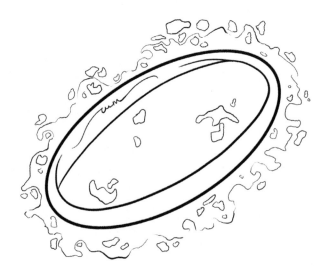

Show us your parody chops and compose your own version of a popular television theme song.[67]

Make it zeitgeisty.

---

[67] Will Smith never sounded as good as he does on "The Fresh Prince of Welfare."

As you're walking down Vine Street, you overhear a few beret-wearing, hemp-tote-bag-toting film students singing the praise of Federico Fellini and prattling on about lens sizes.

In that moment, you decide to write the most pretentious short film ever to exist—one that'll blow their non-prescription glasses right off.

God, we just love Nicholas Cage's acting, don't we?

There's really no one out there who deserves a blockbuster comeback as much as he does.

And you're the one who's going to relaunch his career.

Write something so crazy, so offbeat that only he would sign on to do it.

James Bond is a man of many talents.

Unfortunately, after a workplace sexual harassment case (it was inevitable), he's just been let go from his job at MI6.

What happens next to our beloved 007?[68]

---

[68] Hey, I hear there's an opening to work alongside a certain beloved mall cop at West Orange Pavilion Mall.

It's 1986.

Everyone on the Sunset Strip is wearing at least one form of leather, and hairspray is depleting the ozone layer at unfathomable rates.
Recently released from prison, Johnny/Joan Hog steps out into the midday sun with just a leopard-print shirt on and an eight ball of smack in their pocket, determined to reclaim their role as the wild child of LA's rock scene.

In this episode of *Friends*,[69] the group comes together to finally kill Phoebe.

---

[69] Maybe you've heard of it—the sitcom white people without friends won't shut the fuck up about.

Imagine you've hacked your most hated Hollywood celebrity's Twitter account.

Get them #cancelled with just one tweet.

(Bonus: If you're a real madman/madwoman, do it for real.)[70]

---

[70] For legal purposes, we here at Prompts Gone Wild must make it known that we do (not) condone identity theft or impersonation, no matter how funny it is.

X-Men, but everyone has incredibly lame abilities.[71]

---

[71] Professor Xavier: "Everyone, meet your new classmate, Time Girl. She can tell the time. Any time. *All* the time."

As a joke, the Hollywood Walk of Fame has decided to award a star to the worst actor of all time. Your options:

- Greg Sestero
- Steven Seagal
- Jaden Smith
- Alan Bagh
- Kristen Stewart
- Taylor Lautner
- Tommy Wiseau
- Ruby Rose

Justify your choice.

American Psychoanalyst[72]

---

[72] In this screenplay, your therapist lead hides a secret fetish for seeking retribution against Hollywood's greasy pedophile elites. But will your protagonist be able to keep their deeds a secret forever?

Let your inner voyeur come out to play.

Rewrite *Titanic* from the perspective of a peeping Tom watching Jack and Rose's steamy love affair unfold.[73]

---

[73] For some real fun, make it a series of increasingly erotic journal entries.

In the Bible, Jesus disappeared when he was 12 and didn't reappear until he was 30.

Some say he went backpacking around India. But you know the truth, and you're going to share it in your screenplay about Jesus' lost years.

Prompts Gone Wild presents:

High School Musical:
The Shooting.[74]

---

[74] Troy and company are about to sing a very different tune.

Action films always have the best lines. Using the following set-ups, write your very own quips:

a) The king of a foreign country just got caught red-handed stealing from his subjects.

b) The hero interrupts his masturbation session to shoot the big baddie.

c) A plane crashes into a train, which then crashes into a boat, which then crashes into a parade.

Transcribe your favourite actor's inner monologue[75] as they shop for groceries at Whole Foods.

---

[75] That's the little voice in your head that follows you throughout the day. It's almost like a narrator, but shittier, because it's you.

You're drunk-driving through the Hollywood Hills like a young Lindsay Lohan when you run over what you think is a tourist. You frantically throw them in your trunk before anyone sees.

Only when you hear his beautiful, muffled screaming do you realize it's Timothée Chalamet.

So begins the wildest night of your life.

Goodfellas?

Nah, man, that's so 1990.

What you need is *Soyboys.*[76]

---

[76] What does the mob look like in the current year? My guess is a bunch of hoverboard-riding vegans trying to shake down local butcher shops and meat-eaters. But here's your chance to show us your take!

Crossover films are all the rage these days.

Let's give 'em something they've never seen before by combining two completely different films or franchises.[77]

---

[77] *Step Up* + *Un homme qui dort* = *Step Up 7: The Meaninglessness of Life.*

In a surprising decision, Warner Bros. Pictures has just green-lit your next project:

A WWII frat comedy!

Reimagine all the major WWII players, but as college-aged young adults from rival fraternities.[78]

---

[78] Oh, there's Goebbels now with the beer bong funnel!

An elderly Indiana Jones asks his grandchildren to help him use "The Google" on his smartphone so he can track down the pair of reading glasses he lost last week.[79]

---

[79] Bonus: Write the scene where he tries to get said grandchildren to visit him more often because he's getting lonely.

Make the _____ franchise great again.[80]

---

[80] Please, for the love of god, save us from all these awful reboots by writing a good one. From *Charlie's Angels* to *Pirates of the Caribbean*, you've got so many choices.

You're putting together a crew straight out of *Ocean's Eleven.*

The job: Steal the Buzz Lightyear sex toy from page six.

Like every good movie, this also has to come to an end. But we're goin' out in style.

Write the final battle royale between Godzilla, Gorgo, Gamera, King Kong, and the rest of cinema's greatest mega monsters as they duke it out in the middle of LA!

Get in Touch
Send your wildest responses to
promptsgonewild@gmail.com

Or submit them through promptsgonewild.com
for a chance to be featured on the website and
social media.

DM me on Instagram @promptsgonewild

And whether you loved or hated the book,
let me know by dropping a review online!

#promptsgonewild

Acknowledgements
A special thanks to Ashleigh, Nick, Skylar, and
Makena.

*For more outrageous and uncensored writing prompts,
check out **Writing Prompts Gone Wild** and
Young Adult Prompts Gone Wild. Out now!*

ISBN 978-1-7771927-6-1

51099

Printed in Great Britain
by Amazon

14325553R00078